MARINADE
ENCYCLOPEDIA

*Over 100 recipes for liquid marinades,
sauces & brining liquids*

FIRST EDITION

Printed in China
Marinade Encyclopedia Copyright © 2012 KitchenAdvance
ISBN 978-1-938653-07-0

Table of Contents

About Marinades

A marinade is a seasoned liquid, rub or paste, often acidic, applied to poultry, meats, seafood or vegetables before cooking to add flavor, or to tenderize tougher cuts of meat. Marinades were originally used as preservatives to prevent food from spoiling as quickly, or after spoiling had occurred to hide the unpleasant flavor. The word marinade is derived from the Latin *aqua marina*, meaning from the sea. There are many liquid marinades made from acids such as vinegar, lemon juice, wines, or yogurt, then combined with oils, herbs or spices. The acids soften the texture and cause the meat to cook more quickly. However, the acids can dry out the food, therefore the oils are a necessary part of the marinade, as they add moisture to the food. Though when no oils are used the marinating time is usually shorter. The oils also help hold the aromatic flavors to the food and prevent meats and vegetables from sticking to the pan when cooking. The aromatics may be fresh or dried herbs or spices, onions, garlic or even liqueurs.

Tips for Marinating

When marinating you can either inject or soak the food. When soaking, it is important that poultry, meats and seafood are completely covered, using a container large enough to hold the food, but with minimal extra air. Re-sealable plastic bags are ideal for marinating since most of the air can be squeezed out allowing the marinade to completely surround the meat. Generally 1 cup of marinade to 1 pound of meat is sufficient if using bags, and about 2 cups of marinade if marinating in a flat dish or container. Make sure to turn the meat over or stir several times during the marinating time to insure equal coverage.

Injection marinades are a quick and easy way to marinate meats. The narrow, stainless steel injector needle is used for smoother, liquid marinades, and the wider, plastic injector needles are used for marinades that contain powdered or finely chopped herbs and spices. Before cooking, the marinade is put in the injector and then the needle inserted into the flesh of the meat. The plunger is then displaced and the liquid is injected deep into the meat. While the meat cooks, the marinade produces a strong, concentrated flavor, and without any time spent on marinating.

Generally the recipes in this book would be better suited for the wider, plastic injector, but they can be adapted for the steel, needle tip by substituting minced, fresh ingredients with powdered versions, or first liquefying them in a food processor.

Liquid Marinades, Sauces & Brining Liquids

5-SPICE MARINADE

¼ cup *soy sauce*
¼ cup *dry sherry*
2 tbsp *chili oil*
2 tsp *sesame oil*
2 tsp *5-spice powder*
⅔ cup *green onions, minced*
2 tbsp *ginger, minced*

Yields: ¾ cup

Place soy sauce, sherry, chili oil, sesame oil and 5-spice powder in a small bowl. Whisk to combine. Stir in green onions and ginger.

SUGGESTED USE

Beef, pork or chicken kabobs or satay (1 to 3 hours)

APPLE RUM MARINADE

1 cup *apple juice*
½ cup *soy sauce*
½ cup *honey*
3 tbsp *vegetable oil*
2 cloves *garlic, minced*
½ cup *dark rum*
Pinch *nutmeg*

Yields: 2 cups

Place apple juice, soy sauce, honey, and vegetable oil in a medium bowl. Whisk to combine. Stir in garlic, rum and nutmeg.

SUGGESTED USE

Pork loin, chops or tenderloin (24 hours)
Pork kabobs (4 hours)

ASIAN CITRUS MARINADE

¼ cup *orange juice*
2 tbsp *lemon juice*
2 tbsp *vegetable oil*
2 tsp *hoisin sauce*
2 tsp *hot sauce*

2 tsp *ginger, finely minced*

3 cloves *garlic, minced*

Yields: ⅔ cup

Whisk together the orange and lemon juices in a small bowl. Whisk in the oil and then the hoisin and hot sauce. Stir in the minced ginger and garlic.

SUGGESTED USE

Pork loin (4 to 6 hours)

Pork tenderloin (2 to 4 hours)

Pork chops (4 hours)

Chicken (2 to 4 hours)

Fish fillets (30 to 60 minutes)
Shrimp (1 hour)

ASIAN SESAME MARINADE

½ cup *dry sherry*
2 tbsp *soy sauce*
2 tbsp *vegetable oil*
1 tbsp *sesame oil*
1 tsp *ginger, minced*
1 *green onion, minced*
A pinch *dry red pepper flakes*

Yields: 1 cup

Place sherry, soy sauce, vegetable oil and sesame oil in a medium bowl. Whisk in the ginger, green onion and red pepper flakes.

SUGGESTED USE

Whole chicken (4 to 6 hours)
Boneless chicken breasts (2 to 3 hours)
Shrimp (1 to 3 hours)

BASIL BALSAMIC MARINADE

½ cup *balsamic vinegar*
¼ cup *lemon juice*
⅔ cup *olive oil*
2 cloves *garlic, minced*
¼ cup *parsley, chopped*
¼ cup *basil, chopped*
½ tsp *salt*
¼ tsp *freshly ground pepper*

Yields: 2 cups

Place the vinegar and lemon juice in a medium bowl. Slowly whisk in the olive oil. Stir in the garlic, parsley, basil, salt and pepper.

SUGGESTED USE

Seafood (1 hour)
Boneless chicken breasts (2 to 3 hours)

Mozzarella or goat cheese (1 hour)

BEER MARINADE FOR BEEF

2 cups *beer*

2 tbsp *vegetable oil*

2 tbsp *Worcestershire sauce*

2 tbsp *brown sugar*

½ tsp *pepper*

2 tsp *onion salt*

Yields: 2½ cups

Place all ingredients in a large bowl and whisk to combine.

SUGGESTED USE

Beef roast (12 to 24)
Beef kabobs (12 hours)
Beef steak (8 to 12 hours)

BEER MARINADE WITH ONIONS & SAGE

1 12-ounce *can dark beer*
1 large *onion, sliced*
2 cloves *garlic, minced*
2 tbsp *sugar*
1 tsp *dried sage*
½ tsp *salt*
½ tsp *freshly ground pepper*

Yields: 2 cups

Mix all ingredients in a medium bowl.

SUGGESTED USE

Whole chicken (8 hours)
Beef steak (4 hours)
Pork loin (6 to 8 hours)

BRINING LIQUID FOR PORK

9 cloves *garlic, mashed*
1 quart *water*
½ cup *kosher salt*
2 tbsp *black peppercorns*
6 tbsp *sugar*

1 sprig *fresh thyme*
1 tsp *whole allspice berries*
1 *bay leaf*
2 quarts *ice water*

Yields: 1 gallon

Place garlic, 1 quart water, salt, pepper, sugar, thyme, allspice and bay leaf in a large pot. Bring to a simmer and cook over low heat for 15 minutes. Mix with ice water and cool completely.

SUGGESTED USE

Pork chops or tenderloin (8 to 24 hours)
(Rinse and pat dry after brining and before cooking)

BRINING LIQUID FOR TURKEY

3 cups *water*

½ cup *kosher salt*

¼ cup *sugar*

3 quarts *ice water*

2 sprigs *fresh thyme*

1 tbsp *black peppercorns*

Yields: 1 gallon

Place 3 cups water, salt and sugar in a saucepan and cook over medium heat until the sugar and salt dissolve. Add this mixture to the ice water, add the thyme and pepper.

SUGGESTED USE

Brining a turkey (8 to 12 hours) in a salty liquid before cooking yields a moister, more flavorful cooked bird and infuses the turkey with the flavors of the herbs included. Multiply the brining liquid as needed to cover the turkey completely. Rinse the turkey and pat dry before cooking.

CARIBBEAN MANGO MARINADE

1½ cups or 2 *mangoes, peeled & chopped*
1 whole *habeñero chili (or jalapeño for a more mild marinade)*
1 tbsp *dark rum*
2 cloves *garlic, minced*
1 tbsp *ginger, minced*

½ cup *coconut milk*
¼ cup *lime juice*
2 tbsp *cilantro, chopped*
½ tsp *salt*

Yields: 2½ cups

Place the mango, chili and rum in the food processor and puree. Combine with garlic, and ginger, in a medium saucepan and bring to a boil. Reduce heat and simmer for 15-20 minutes. Removed from heat and cool. Stir in the coconut milk, lime juice and cilantro and salt.

SUGGESTED USE

Shrimp or scallops (2 hours)
Boneless chicken breasts (4 to 6 hours)
Chicken pieces (3 to 4 hours)

CARIBBEAN RUM-LIME MARINADE

½ cup *lime juice*
¼ cup *dark rum*
2 tbsp *brown sugar*
2 tbsp *vegetable oil*
2 cloves *garlic, minced*
½ tsp *ground allspice*
Pinch *red pepper flakes*

Yields: ⅔ cup

Place the lime juice and rum in a medium mixing bowl. Whisk in the vegetable oil, garlic, allspice, brown sugar and red pepper flakes.

SUGGESTED USE

Pork tenderloin (2 to 3 hours)
Pork or chicken kabobs (2 hours)

Jumbo shrimp (1 to 2 hours)

14

CHILI PASTE MARINADE

2 tbsp *garlic, minced*

1 tbsp *ginger, minced*
⅓ cup *hoisin sauce*
¼ cup *rice wine vinegar*
2 tbsp *lemon juice*

2 tbsp *sesame oil*

¼ cup *sugar*

¼ cup *soy sauce*

2 tbsp *Thai chili paste*

¼ cup *green onions, chopped*

¼ cup *cilantro, chopped*

1 tsp *freshly ground pepper*

½ cup *vegetable oil*

Yields: 2 cups

Place garlic, ginger, hoisin, vinegar, lemon juice, sesame oil, sugar, soy sauce and chili paste in the food processor. Process to puree. Add the green onions, cilantro and pepper and process to a chunky puree. With machine running add the oil.

SUGGESTED USE

Top sirloin, skirt or flank steak (4 hours)

Chicken (2 to 3 hours)

CHIMICHURRI SAUCE

½ cup *olive oil*

¼ cup *red wine vinegar*

1 small *onion, minced*

⅓ cup *parsley, finely chopped*

4 cloves *garlic, minced*

1 tbsp *fresh oregano, finely chopped*

½ tsp *salt*

¼ tsp *cayenne pepper*

¼ tsp *freshly ground pepper*

Yields: 1 cup

Place olive oil and vinegar in a medium bowl. Whisk together and then stir in the rest of the ingredients. Let stand at room temperature for 1-2 hours before using as a marinade or as a sauce.

SUGGESTED USE

Top sirloin or other cuts of beef (2 to 4 hours)

CHINESE BBQ MARINADE

¼ cup *dry sherry*

2 tbsp *soy sauce*

3 tbsp *hoisin sauce*

3 tbsp *ketchup (page 100)*

1 tbsp *vegetable oil*

2 tbsp *sugar*

2 cloves *garlic, minced*

1 tbsp *ginger, minced*

4 *green onions, minced*

¼ tsp *freshly ground pepper*

Yields: 1 cup

Place sherry, soy sauce, hoisin sauce, ketchup, vegetable oil and sugar in a medium bowl. Whisk to combine. Add the garlic, ginger, green onions and pepper. Stir to mix together.

SUGGESTED USE

Pork tenderloin (3 to 4 hours)

Boneless chicken breasts (2 to 3 hours)

CILANTRO LIME MARINADE

½ cup *lime juice*

3 cloves *garlic, minced*

½ cup *cilantro, chopped*

2 tbsp *olive oil*

½ tsp *dried red pepper flakes*

½ tsp *salt*

Yields: 1 cup

Place lime juice, garlic, cilantro, olive oil, red pepper flakes, and salt in a medium bowl. Whisk to combine well.

SUGGESTED USE

Shrimp (1 hour)
Chicken (2 to 3 hours)

CILANTRO & WHITE WINE MARINADE

½ cup *dry white wine*

¼ cup *lime juice*

2 tbsp *olive oil*

2 tbsp *cilantro, minced*

¼ tsp *ground pepper*

¼ tsp *salt*

Yields: ½ cup

Place white wine, lime juice, and olive oil in a small bowl, and whisk to combine. Stir in remaining ingredients.

SUGGESTED USE

Firm fish fillets (1 to 2 hours)
Chicken breasts (2 to 4 hours)

CITRUS MARINADE

2 cloves *garlic, sliced*
⅓ cup *olive oil*
3 tbsp *dark brown sugar*
2 tbsp *balsamic vinegar*
1½ tsp *Dijon mustard*
¼ cup *lemon juice*
¼ cup *orange juice*
1½ tsp *lemon zest*
½ tsp *salt*
¼ tsp *freshly ground pepper*

Yields: 1 cup

Combine all ingredients in a medium bowl.

SUGGESTED USE

Shrimp (1 to 3 hours)
Chicken pieces or boneless chicken breasts (2 to 3 hours)

CRANBERRY MARINADE

1 cup *cranberries*

½ cup *water*

1½ tsp *orange zest*

3 tbsp *red wine vinegar*

2 tbsp *shallots, finely chopped*

½ cup *golden brown sugar*

2 tsp *salt*

½ tsp *freshly ground pepper*
¼ cup *vegetable oil*

Yields: 1½ cups

Place cranberries, water and orange zest in a medium saucepan. Bring to a boil and then reduce heat and simmer until cranberries burst, stirring occasionally, about 10 minutes. Puree until smooth in food processor. Add vinegar, shallots, sugar, salt and pepper and blend well. Gradually whisk in oil. Cool completely.

SUGGESTED USE

Pork loin or tenderloin (8 to 24 hours)
Chicken (6 to 8 hours)

CUBAN MOJO MARINADE

¼ cup *olive oil*

3 tbsp *orange juice*

3 tbsp *lime juice*

6 cloves *garlic, minced*

1 *serrano chili, minced*

½ tsp *ground cumin*

½ tsp *salt*

Yields: ¾ cup

Whisk together the olive oil, orange juice and lime juice in a medium bowl. Whisk in the garlic, chili, cumin and salt.

SUGGESTED USE

Mojo sauce is great for marinating as well as served on meat.

Pork (2 to 4 hours)

Chicken (1 to 3 hours)

CURRIED GINGER MARINADE

⅓ cup *olive oil*

3 tbsp *lime juice*

2 tbsp *soy sauce*

1 tbsp *honey*

1 tsp *garlic, minced*

1 tsp *ginger, minced*

½ cup *cilantro, chopped*

1 tsp *curry powder*

½ tsp *salt*
¼ tsp *freshly ground pepper*

Yields: 1 cup

Place all ingredients in a blender or food processor and puree.

SUGGESTED USE

Swordfish or other firm-fleshed fish (30 minutes to 2 hours)

Shrimp (30 to 60 minutes)
Boneless chicken breasts (1 to 2 hours)

CURRY MARINADE

1 large *onion, chopped*

6 cloves *garlic, minced*

½ cup *soy sauce*

¼ cup *cider vinegar*

2 tbsp *vegetable oil*

1 tbsp *brown sugar*

2 tsp *curry powder*

½ tsp *freshly ground pepper*

Yields: 1½ cups

Place onion, garlic, soy sauce, vinegar, oil, brown sugar, curry powder, and pepper in a medium bowl. Stir to combine well and dissolve the sugar.

SUGGESTED USE

Pork loin (12 to 24 hours)
Pork tenderloin or chops (6 to 8 hours)
Turkey breast (8 to 12 hours)

FAJITA MARINADE

1 12-ounce *can beer*

2 tbsp *vegetable oil*

¼ cup *lime juice*

½ *onion, sliced*

2 *jalapeños, seeded & sliced*

4 cloves *garlic, minced*

1 *bay leaf*

1 tbsp *chili powder*

1 tsp *ground cumin*

1 tsp *freshly ground pepper*

½ tsp *salt*

Yields: 2 cups

Place the beer, vegetable oil, lime juice, onion, garlic, bay leaf, jalapenos, chili powder, cumin, salt and pepper in a large bowl. Stir to combine well.

SUGGESTED USE

Beef top sirloin (up to 24 hours)
Chicken pieces on the bone (up to 12 hours)
Boneless chicken breasts (3 to 4 hours)
Chicken kabobs (2 to 3 hours)
Shrimp (1 to 2 hours)

25

GARLIC LIME MARINADE

6 large *cloves garlic, minced*

2 tbsp *soy sauce*

2 tbsp *ginger, minced*

2 tsp *Dijon mustard*

⅓ cup *lime juice*

½ cup *olive oil*
Pinch *cayenne pepper*

Yields: 1 cup

Place garlic, soy sauce, ginger, mustard, lime juice, olive oil and cayenne in a blender or food processor. Blend to puree.

SUGGESTED USE

Pork tenderloin (6 to 8 hours)

Chicken breasts (2 to 3 hours)
Fish fillets (1 hour)

GARLIC SOY MARINADE

¼ cup *soy sauce*
¼ cup *medium-dry sherry*

1 tbsp *vegetable oil*

2 tbsp *brown sugar*

2 cloves *garlic, minced*

1 tbsp *ginger, minced*
¼ tsp *freshly ground pepper*

Yields: ¾ cup

Whisk together all ingredients.

SUGGESTED USE

Boneless chicken breasts (1 hour)
Pork tenderloin (2 hours)
Shrimp (1 hour)

GEORGIAN MARINADE

4 juicing *oranges*

2 *lemons*

½ cup *dry white wine*

2 *shallots, minced*

2 cloves *garlic, minced*
1 tbsp *ginger, minced*

2 tbsp *paprika*

½ tbsp *olive oil*

1 tsp *sugar*

1 tsp *black peppercorns, cracked*

½ tsp *salt*
2 *cinnamon sticks*

Yields: 1½ cups

Zest one lemon and one orange. Juice all of the oranges and lemons. Combine the orange juice, lemon juice and wine in a saucepan and boil until only ½ cup of the liquid remains and let cool. Combine the shallots, garlic and ginger in a bowl. Stir in the reduced juice, zest, paprika, oil, sugar, peppercorns, salt and cinnamon sticks.

SUGGESTED USE

Shrimp or scallops (1 to 2 hours)
Chicken pieces or whole chicken (2 to 3 hours)

GINGER ORANGE MARINADE

½ cup *orange juice*
2 tbsp *sesame oil*
2 tbsp *ginger, minced*
1 tbsp *orange zest*
1 tsp *rice wine vinegar*
Pinch *cayenne pepper*
Pinch *sugar*

Yields: ¾ cup

Place orange juice and sesame oil in a small bowl. Whisk to combine. Stir in ginger, orange zest, vinegar, cayenne and sugar.

SUGGESTED USE

Swordfish or other firm fish fillets (30 to 60 minutes)
Boneless chicken breasts (1 to 3 hours)

GINGER TERIYAKI MARINADE

½ cup *soy sauce*

½ cup *dry white wine*

¼ cup *sake or dry sherry*

¼ cup *sugar*

2 slices *ginger*

2 tbsp *water*

1 tbsp *cornstarch*

Yields: 1 cup

Place the soy sauce, wine, sake (or sherry), sugar and ginger slices in a 2-quart saucepan. Bring mixture to a boil; then simmer 5 minutes. Stir together water and cornstarch and whisk into sauce. Stir over medium heat for 1 minute or until thickened. Strain sauce and cool completely.

SUGGESTED USE

Delicious as a marinade, a glaze or a dipping sauce.

Boneless chicken breasts (2 to 4 hours)

Chicken kabobs (2 hours)

Beef steaks (2 to 4 hours)

Beef kabobs (2 to 3 hours)

Shrimp (1 hour)
Firm fish fillets (30 to 90 minutes)

GRAPEFRUIT MARINADE

1 cup *grapefruit juice*

½ cup *dry sherry*

2 tbsp *sesame oil*

¼ tsp *cayenne pepper*
¼ tsp *salt*

Yields: 1½ cups

Place all ingredients into a medium bowl and whisk to combine.

SUGGESTED USE

Fish fillets (2 to 4 hours)

HERBES DE PROVENCE MARINADE

¼ cup *lemon juice*

1 tbsp *lemon zest*

¼ cup *dry white wine*

2 tbsp *sherry vinegar*

½ cup *olive oil*

2 tbsp *Herbs de Provence*

3 cloves *garlic, minced*

1 tbsp *rosemary, minced*

½ tsp *salt*

½ tsp *freshly ground pepper*

Yields: 2 cups

Place the lemon juice, zest, white wine and vinegar in a medium bowl. Slowly whisk in the oil. Stir in the Herbs de Provence, garlic, fresh rosemary, salt and pepper.

SUGGESTED USE

Tuna or other stronger fish fillets (2 to 3 hours)
Whole chicken or chicken pieces (2 to 4 hours)

HOISIN BBQ SAUCE

1 cup *hoisin sauce*

2 tbsp *dry sherry*

2 tbsp *sesame oil*

1 tbsp *sugar*

1½ tsp *rice wine vinegar*

Yields: 1 cup

Place all ingredients in a medium bowl and whisk to combine.

SUGGESTED USE

Use this as a marinade or a basting sauce.
Pork spareribs (8 hours)

Chicken drumsticks (2 hours)
Boneless chicken breasts (30 minutes)

HONEY DIJON MARINADE

¼ cup *Dijon mustard*
¼ cup *honey*
2 tbsp *vegetable oil*
2 tsp *freshly ground pepper*
1 tsp *curry powder*

Yields: ½ cup

Whisk all together in a medium bowl.

SUGGESTED USE

Whole chicken (4 to 6 hours)
(Loosen the skin across the breast, thigh and leg and work the marinade under the skin all over the chicken. Rub any extra marinade over the skin to moisten.)
Boneless chicken breasts (2 hours)

Shrimp (30 minutes)

Pork tenderloin (2 to 4 hours)

HONEY HOISIN MARINADE

¼ cup *soy sauce*

⅓ *cup honey*

2 tbsp *hoisin sauce*
2 tbsp *dry sherry*

2 tbsp *rice wine vinegar*

2 cloves *garlic, minced*
2 tbsp *ginger, minced*

½ tsp *crushed red pepper flakes*

Yields: 1½ cups

Place all ingredients in a medium bowl. Stir to combine well.

SUGGESTED USE

Chicken wings (6 to 8 hours)
Pork spareribs (8 to 12 hours)

HONEY LEMON MARINADE

½ cup *onion, finely chopped*

6 tbsp *lemon juice*

1 tsp *lemon zest*

2 tbsp *vegetable oil*

2 tbsp *honey*

¼ tsp *freshly ground pepper*
½ tsp *salt*

Yields: 1 cup

Place onion and lemon juice in a small bowl. Stir to combine. Add vegetable oil, honey, lemon zest, salt and pepper and stir to combine.

SUGGESTED USE

Boneless chicken breasts or kabobs (2 to 3 hours)
Shrimp (1 to 3 hours)
Firm fish fillets (1 hour)

HONEY PLUM BBQ MARINADE

⅓ cup *lemon juice*

¼ cup *honey*

1 cup *tomato sauce*

¼ cup *plum jam*

2 tbsp *vegetable oil*

1 tsp *paprika*
1 tsp *hot sauce*

Yields: 2 cups

Combine all ingredients in a medium saucepan. Bring mixture to boil, stirring often over medium heat. Reduce heat and simmer 5 minutes. Add more hot sauce to taste. Cool before using.

SUGGESTED USE

This can be used as a marinade, a baste, or even a table sauce.

Pork chops or tenderloins (2 to 4 hours)
Chicken pieces (2 to 4 hours)

INDONESIAN SPICY HONEY MARINADE

¼ cup *honey*

2 tbsp *soy sauce*

1 tbsp *molasses*

¼ cup *lemon juice*

2 tbsp *lime juice*

1 tbsp *rice wine vinegar*

⅓ cup *vegetable oil*

3 serrano *chilies, minced*

½ tsp *cumin*

1 tbsp *ginger, minced*

Yields: 1½ cups

Place honey, soy sauce, molasses, lemon juice, lime juice and rice wine vinegar in a medium bowl. Whisk in the oil slowly. Stir in the chilies, cumin, and ginger.

SUGGESTED USE

Chicken wings (6 to 8 hours)

Cornish game hens (8 to 12 hours)

Pork spareribs (8 to 24 hours)

ITALIAN MARINADE

⅓ cup *balsamic vinegar*

¼ cup *lemon juice*

2 *anchovies, finely chopped*

⅔ cup *olive oil*

4 cloves *garlic, minced*

1 tbsp *capers*

2 green *onions, minced*

¼ cup *parsley, chopped*

½ tsp *freshly ground pepper*

Yields: 1½ cups

Place the vinegar, lemon juice and anchovies in a medium bowl. Slowly whisk in the olive oil. Stir in the garlic, capers, green onions, parsley and pepper.

SUGGESTED USE

Vegetables (1 hour)
Boneless chicken breasts (2 to 3 hours)

Shrimp (1 to 3 hours)
Fish fillets (2 hours)

JAMAICAN JERK MARINADE

¼ cup *lime juice*

¼ cup *olive oil*

¼ cup *dark rum*

¼ cup *golden brown sugar*

¼ cup *soy sauce*

2 tsp *hot sauce*

1 tsp *ground nutmeg*

½ tsp *ground allspice*

½ tsp *ground cinnamon*

¼ cup *cilantro, chopped*

2 tbsp *ginger, finely minced.*

Yields: 1 cup

Place lime juice, olive oil, rum, brown sugar, soy sauce and hot sauce in a medium bowl. Whisk to combine. Mix in spices, cilantro and ginger.

SUGGESTED USE

Pork tenderloin (6 to 8 hours)

Chicken (2 hours)

Shrimp (1 hour)

JAPANESE MARINADE

⅓ cup *sake*

3 tbsp *mirin*

¼ cup *soy sauce*

¼ cup *dry white wine or rice wine vinegar*

1 tbsp *brown sugar*

1 tbsp *vegetable oil*

Yields: 1 cup

Place all ingredients in a small bowl. Whisk to combine.

SUGGESTED USE

Shrimp (1 to 2 hours)
Boneless chicken breasts (1 to 2 hours)
Pork kabobs or satay (1 to 2 hours)

KOREAN BBQ MARINADE

¾ cup *soy sauce*
2 tbsp *vegetable oil*
1 tsp *sesame oil*
2 tbsp *dry sherry*
2 tbsp *lime juice*
2 tbsp *dark brown sugar*
6 green *onions, finely chopped*
5 cloves *garlic, minced*
1 tbsp *sesame seeds, toasted*
¼ tsp *freshly ground pepper*

Yields: 1 cup

Place soy sauce, both oils, sherry, lime juice, and brown sugar in a medium bowl. Whisk to combine. Stir in green onions, garlic, sesame seeds and pepper.

SUGGESTED USE

Beef top sirloin or top round (3 to 4 hours)
Cubes or strips of sirloin (1 hour)
(marinated & skewered before cooking)
Pork spareribs (8 hours)

LEMON BBQ MARINADE

½ cup *lemon juice*
1 tsp *lemon zest*
⅓ cup *vegetable oil*
2 tsp *Dijon mustard*
3 tbsp *green onions, thinly sliced*
4 tsp *sugar*
1 tsp *salt*
¼ tsp *freshly ground pepper*

Yields: 1 cup

Place lemon juice, zest, oil, and mustard in a medium bowl. Whisk to combine. Stir in green onions, sugar, salt and pepper.

SUGGESTED USE

Leg of lamb (24 hours)
Boneless chicken breasts (1 to 3 hours)
Fish fillets (30 to 60 minutes)

LEMON DILL MARINADE

⅔ cup *lemon juice*
¼ cup *olive oil*
2 tbsp *dill, minced*
½ tsp *salt*
¼ tsp *freshly ground white pepper*

Yields: 1 cup

Place all ingredients in a small bowl and whisk to combine.

SUGGESTED USE

Fish Fillets (30 to 60 minutes)
Shrimp (30 to 60 minutes)

LEMON HERB FISH MARINADE

1½ cups *dry white wine*
½ cup *lemon juice*
1 tbsp *lemon zest*
½ cup *olive oil*
3 cloves *garlic, minced*
2 tbsp *parsley, minced*
2 tbsp *basil, minced*
1 tsp *rosemary, chopped*
½ tsp *salt*
¼ tsp *ground white pepper*

Yields: 2½ cups

Place wine, lemon juice, and zest in medium bowl. Slowly whisk in the olive oil. Stir in the garlic, herbs, salt and pepper.

SUGGESTED USE

Fish steaks or fillets (2 to 4 hours)
Shrimp (2 to 4 hours)

45

LEMON-LIME MARINADE

¾ cup *lemon juice*
1 tsp *lemon zest*
¾ cup *lime juice*
1 tsp *lime zest*
2 tbsp *sugar*
2 cloves *garlic, minced*
½ tsp *cayenne pepper*
½ tsp *salt*
¼ cup *vegetable oil*

Yields: 1½ cups

Combine everything but the oil in a medium saucepan and simmer for 5 minutes, stirring often. Whisk in the oil and let cool completely.

SUGGESTED USE

Chicken pieces (4 hours)
Boneless chicken breasts (2 to 3 hours)
Shrimp (1 to 2 hours)

LEMON PEPPER MARINADE

¼ cup *lemon juice*
½ tsp *dried red pepper flakes*
1 tsp *coarsely ground black pepper*
½ tsp *salt*
1 tbsp *lemon zest*
3 cloves *garlic, minced*
¼ cup *parsley, coarsely chopped*
2 tbsp *oregano, coarsely chopped*
½ *cup olive oil*

Yields: 1 cup

Place lemon juice, red pepper flakes, pepper and salt in a medium bowl. Whisk until salt is dissolved. Add lemon zest, garlic, parsley, and oregano. Whisk in olive oil.

SUGGESTED USE

Chicken (2 to 3 hours)
Shrimp (3 to 4 hours)
Fish fillets (1 hour)

LEMON SOY MARINADE

⅔ cup *soy sauce*
½ cup *lemon juice*
2 tsp *lemon zest*
1 tbsp *Dijon mustard*
2 cloves *garlic, minced*
½ cup *vegetable oil*
½ tsp *ground black pepper*

Yields: 2 cups

Place soy sauce, lemon juice and lemon zest in a medium bowl. Whisk to combine. Whisk in the mustard, garlic, oil and pepper.

SUGGESTED USE

Fish fillets (2 hours)
Shrimp (2 hours)

LEMON VODKA MARINADE

¼ cup *vodka*
⅓ cup *lemon zest*
¼ cup *vegetable oil*
¼ cup *olive oil*
¼ cup *dill, chopped*
¼ cup *green onions, chopped*
½ tsp *salt*
¼ tsp *ground white pepper*

Yields: 1½ cups

Place the vodka, lemon zest in a medium bowl. Slowly whisk in the oils. Stir in the dill, green onions, salt and pepper.

SUGGESTED USE

Fish fillets, like salmon or tuna (2 to 3 hours)

MADEIRA MARINADE

½ cup *sherry or white wine vinegar*
1 cup *Madeira wine*
¼ cup *olive oil*
¼ cup *shallots, chopped*
1 clove *garlic, minced*
1 tbsp *Herbes de Provence*
1 tbsp *whole peppercorns*

Yields: 1½ cups

Place vinegar and wine in a medium bowl. Slowly whisk in the olive oil. Stir in the remaining ingredients.

SUGGESTED USE

London broil (6 to 8 hours)

MAPLE BOURBON MARINADE

1 cup *maple syrup*
½ cup *bourbon*
½ cup *cider vinegar*
½ cup *orange juice*
1 tbsp *orange zest*
1 tbsp *dark brown sugar*
2 tbsp *Dijon mustard*
2 tbsp *vegetable oil*

Yields: 1¾ cups

Place the ingredients in a medium bowl. Whisk in the oil.

SUGGESTED USE

Pork chops or tenderloin (2 hours)
Chicken wings (4 hours)
Pork spareribs (6 hours)

MARGARITA MARINADE

3 tbsp *tequila*
2 tbsp *triple sec*
3 tbsp *lime juice*
¼ cup *vegetable oil*
1 large jalapeño *chili, seeded, minced*
1½ tsp *lime zest*
1 tsp *chili powder*
½ tsp *salt*

Yields: ¾ cup

Whisk together tequila, triple sec, lime juice and vegetable oil in a medium bowl. Stir in the jalapeño, lime zest, chili powder, and salt.

SUGGESTED USE

Shrimp (30 to 60 minutes)
Boneless chicken breasts (1 to 3 hours)
Chicken pieces (3 to 4 hours)

MAYONNAISE

1 *egg*
2 tsp *sea salt*
2 tbsp *cider vinegar*
¼ cup *grapeseed oil*
¾ cup *extra virgin olive oil*

Yields: 1 cup

This recipe can be made with an immersion blender, food processor, or by mixing with a whisk by hand, but be extra careful to ensure the oil emulsifies, as stated in the instructions below. All steps should be using the blender, processor or whisk.

Mix together egg yolk, sea salt and cider vinegar until smooth and light in color. Extremely slowly, start mixing in the oil, drop by drop - you will see the mixture begin to emulsify. Continue adding the oil very slowly until the mixture thickens and is no longer liquid. Once it has become thicker and is clearly emulsifying, you can begin to add the oil a bit more quickly.

MINT & GARLIC MARINADE

⅔ cup *mint, chopped*
2 cloves *garlic, minced*
¼ cup *lemon juice*
½ cup *olive oil*
½ tsp *salt*
¼ tsp *freshly ground pepper*

Yields: 1 cup

Place mint, garlic, and lemon juice in food processor and pulse to finely chop. With the machine running add the olive oil in a thin stream. Add the salt and pepper and let stand 1 hour before using as a marinade.

SUGGESTED USE

Leg of lamb (8 hours)
Lamb chops (2 to 3 hours)
Lamb kabobs (2 to 4 hours)

MINTY LEMON MARINADE

¼ cup *dry white wine*
⅓ cup *lemon juice*
1 tbsp *lemon zest*
½ cup *olive oil*
¼ cup *mint, chopped*
3 tbsp *shallots, minced*
½ tsp *salt*
¼ tsp *freshly ground pepper*

Yields: 1½ cups

Place the wine, lemon juice and zest in a medium bowl. Whisk in the olive oil. Stir in the mint, shallots, salt and pepper.

SUGGESTED USE

Boneless chicken breasts (2 hours)
Lamb chops or kabobs (4 to 6 hours)

MOROCCAN RED PEPPER MARINADE

4 tsp *coriander seeds*
1 tbsp *cumin seeds*
½ tsp *turmeric*
2 7-ounce *jars roasted red peppers, well drained*
⅓ cup *onion, chopped*
3 cloves *garlic, peeled*
¼ cup *honey*
¼ cup *lime juice*
1 tbsp *lime zest*
¼ cup *olive oil*
½ tsp *salt*
¼ tsp *freshly ground pepper*

Yields: 2 cups

In a small skillet, lightly toast the coriander, cumin and turmeric over medium heat until fragrant. Transfer to a food processor and add red pepper, onion and garlic. Puree until smooth. Add honey, lime juice, and zest, and, with the processor running, pour in oil. Add the salt and pepper.

SUGGESTED USE

This marinade can also be used as a sauce.
Shrimp (30 to 60 minutes)
Boneless chicken breasts (1 to 3 hours)

MUSTARD GINGER MARINADE

⅓ cup *sherry vinegar*
2 tbsp *soy sauce*
1 tbsp *coarse-grained mustard*
1 tbsp *honey*
⅓ cup *vegetable oil*
2 tbsp *ginger, minced*
2 cloves *garlic, minced*
1 tbsp *shallots, minced*
½ tsp *salt*
¼ tsp *ground pepper*

Yields: 1 cup

Place vinegar, soy sauce, mustard, and honey in a medium bowl. Whisk in oil and then stir in ginger, garlic, shallots, salt and pepper.

SUGGESTED USE

Salmon steaks (2 to 3 hours)
Boneless chicken breasts (2 hours)
Chicken pieces (4 hours)
Pork chops or pork tenderloin (6 hours)

ORANGE ACHIOTE MARINADE

½ cup *lime juice*
1 cup *orange juice*
¼ cup *vegetable oil*
¾ cup *achiote paste*
½ cup *red onion, chopped*
4 cloves *garlic, minced*
½ cup *cilantro, chopped*
2 tbsp *dried oregano*
⅛ tsp *cayenne pepper*
½ tsp *salt*
¼ tsp *freshly ground pepper*

Yields: 1½ cups

Place all ingredients in a food processor or blender and puree until very thick.

SUGGESTED USE

Turkey (8 to 10 hours)
Chicken pieces (4 to 6 hours)
Boneless chicken breasts (2 to 3 hours)
Shrimp (4 to 6 hours)

ORANGE ASIAN HONEY MARINADE

½ cup *orange juice*
½ tsp *orange zest*
¼ cup *honey*
¼ cup *rice wine vinegar*
½ tsp *ginger, minced*

Yields: 1 cup

Combine all ingredients in a medium mixing bowl and mix well.

SUGGESTED USE

Pork chops or loin (8 to 24 hours)
Chicken (3 to 4 hours)

ORANGE BOURBON BBQ SAUCE

¼ cup *vegetable oil*
1 large *onion, minced*
⅔ cup *Bourbon*
⅔ cup *ketchup (page 100)*
½ cup *cider vinegar*
½ cup *orange juice*
½ cup *maple syrup*
⅓ cup *dark molasses*
2 tbsp *Worcestershire sauce*
½ tsp *salt*
¼ tsp *freshly ground pepper*

Yields: 1½ cups

Heat oil in a 4-quart saucepan and cook onions until tender, about 6 minutes. Add the Bourbon, ketchup, vinegar, orange juice, maple syrup, molasses, Worcestershire, salt and pepper. Bring to a boil, stirring frequently. Reduce heat to low and simmer until mixture thickens, about 30 minutes.

SUGGESTED USE

Use some of the sauce for basting and more when serving.
Pork spareribs (12 hours)
Chicken pieces (4 hours)
Boneless chicken breasts (2 hours)

ORANGE MAPLE MARINADE

1 cup *orange juice*
¼ cup *maple syrup*
2 tbsp *vegetable oil*
4 cloves *garlic, minced*
½ tsp *dried thyme*
½ tsp *salt*

Yields: 1½ cups

Place orange juice, maple syrup and vegetable oil in a medium bowl. Whisk to combine. Stir in the garlic, thyme, and salt.

SUGGESTED USE

Pork ribs (6 to 24 hours)
Pork tenderloin (4 to 6 hours)
Boneless chicken breasts (2 to 3 hours)

ORANGE PEPPER MARINADE

½ cup *orange juice*
2 tbsp *vegetable oil*
2 tbsp *freshly finely ground black pepper*
¼ tsp *chili powder*
½ tsp *salt*
2 tbsp *cilantro, chopped*

Yields: ¾ cup

Place the orange juice, vegetable oil, pepper, chili powder, and salt in a medium bowl. Whisk to combine. Stir in cilantro.

SUGGESTED USE

Pork tenderloin or chop (2 to 4 hours)
Chicken pieces (4 to 6 hours)

Boneless chicken breasts (1 to 2 hours)

ORANGE SOY MARINADE

¼ cup *soy sauce*
1 cup *orange juice*
2 tbsp *lemon juice*
2 tbsp *ketchup (page 100)*
2 tbsp *vegetable oil*
2 cloves *garlic, minced*

Yields: 1½ cup

Place all ingredients in a medium bowl and whisk together.

SUGGESTED USE

Boneless chicken breasts (2 hours)
Chicken pieces on the bone (2 to 4 hours)
Whole chickens & Cornish Game Hens (up to 24 hours)
Fish fillets (20 minutes to 1 hour)

ORANGE SOY STEAK MARINADE

2 cups *orange juice*
¼ cup *soy sauce*
2 tbsp *vegetable oil*
4 cloves *garlic, minced*
1 tsp *freshly ground pepper*
½ tsp *cumin*
½ tsp *salt*

Yields: 2½ cups

Place the orange juice and soy sauce in a medium bowl. Whisk in the oil. Stir in the garlic, pepper, cumin and salt.

SUGGESTED USE

Beef skirt steak or top sirloin (6 to 24 hours)

PINEAPPLE CHILI MARINADE

½ cup *pineapple juice, unsweetened*
¼ cup *lime juice*
2 tbsp *soy sauce*
2 tbsp *chili powder*
⅓ cup *dry white wine*
⅓ cup *vegetable oil*
2 tbsp *jalapeño, diced & seeded*
¼ cup *red onion, chopped*
¼ cup *pineapple, dicèd*
¼ cup *cilantro, chopped*
½ tsp *salt*

Yields: 2½ cups

Place the pineapple juice, lime juice, soy sauce, chili powder, and wine in a medium bowl. Slowly whisk in the oil. Stir in the jalapeño, red onion, pineapple, cilantro and salt.

SUGGESTED USE

Shrimp (2 hours)
Fish fillets (1 hour)
Boneless chicken breast (2 hours)
Pork chops or tenderloin (3 to 4 hours)

POLLO ASADO MARINADE

¾ cup *apple juice*
3 tbsp *lime juice*
2 tbsp *vegetable oil*
3 cloves *garlic, minced*
1 *serrano or jalapeño chili, minced*
1 tsp *paprika*
½ tsp *cayenne pepper*
½ tsp *dried oregano*
½ tsp *salt*
½ tsp *freshly ground pepper*

Yields: 1¼ cups

Place apple juice, lime juice, oil, garlic, chili, paprika, cayenne, oregano, salt and pepper in medium bowl. Whisk to combine well.

SUGGESTED USE

Boneless chicken (1 to 4 hours)
Chicken pieces (1 to 4 hours)

PORT WINE MARINADE

1½ cups *ruby port*
⅓ cup *balsamic vinegar*
1 tbsp *lemon juice*
½ cup *olive oil*
2 tbsp *shallots, minced*
2 cloves *garlic, minced*
3 tbsp *sage, chopped*
½ tsp *salt*
½ tsp *freshly ground pepper*

Yields: 2½ cups

Place port, vinegar, and lemon juice in a medium bowl. Slowly whisk in the oil. Stir in the remaining ingredients.

SUGGESTED USE

Beef tenderloin (6 to 8 hours)
Beef kabobs (4 to 6 hours)

RASPBERRY MARINADE

1 cup *raspberries (fresh or frozen)*
¼ cup *sugar*
3 tbsp *raspberry or red wine vinegar*
2 tbsp *vegetable oil*
1 tbsp *Dijon mustard*

Yields: ½ cup

Place the raspberries, sugar and vinegar in a 2-quart saucepan. Bring to a simmer, stirring until raspberries fall apart. Whisk in the oil and mustard and set aside to cool completely before using as a marinade.

SUGGESTED USE

Pork tenderloin (2 to 4 hours)
Pork chops (2 to 4 hours)
Spareribs (8 to 24 hours)
Chicken pieces on the bone (4 to 8 hours)
Cornish Game Hen (6 to 8 hours)

RED WINE & GARLIC MARINADE

1 cup *dry red wine*
4 cloves *garlic, minced*
2 tbsp *dried oregano*
1 tbsp *dried rosemary*
2 tsp *coarsely ground pepper*
½ tsp *salt*

Yields: 1 cup

Place red wine, garlic, oregano, rosemary, salt and pepper in a large bowl. Whisk together to combine.

SUGGESTED USE

Leg of lamb or boned & butterflied leg of lamb (8 to 24 hours)
London broil (8 to 24 hours)
Top sirloin (6 to 8 hours)

RED WINE & HERB MARINADE

1¼ cups *dry red wine*
4 tbsp *olive oil*
¼ cup *onion, finely chopped*
1 clove *garlic, minced*
1 tbsp *parsley, chopped*
1 tsp *thyme*
1 *bay leaf*
½ tsp *salt*
¼ tsp *freshly ground pepper*

Yields: 1½ cups

Mix all ingredients in a medium bowl.

SUGGESTED USE

London broil or roast (6 to 8 hours or overnight)

Leg of lamb (6 to 8 hours)

ROSEMARY BALSAMIC MARINADE

2 cloves *garlic, minced*
1 tbsp *rosemary, minced*
¼ cup *olive oil*
4 tbsp *balsamic vinegar*
½ tsp *salt*
¼ tsp *freshly ground pepper*

Yields: ½ cup

Place garlic, rosemary, olive oil, balsamic vinegar, salt and pepper in a small bowl. Whisk to combine well.

SUGGESTED USE

Boneless chicken breasts (30 to 60 minutes)
Chicken pieces on the bones (2 to 3 hours)
Skewered shrimp (1 hour)

Chicken or turkey kabobs (2 hours)

ROSEMARY-DIJON MARINADE

3 tbsp *Dijon mustard*
2 tbsp *white wine vinegar*
2 tbsp *olive oil*
2 tsp *rosemary, minced or*
½ tsp *dried rosemary*
2 cloves *garlic, minced*
¼ tsp *freshly ground pepper*
¼ tsp *salt*

Yields: ½ cup

Place mustard, vinegar and olive oil in a medium bowl. Whisk to combine. Whisk in rosemary, garlic, salt and pepper.

SUGGESTED USE

Lamb chops or kabobs (6 to 8 hours)
Turkey breast (6 to 8 hours)
Turkey kabobs (3 to 4 hours)
Skewered vegetables (1 hour)

SESAME ORANGE MARINADE

¼ cup *soy sauce*
2 tbsp *cider vinegar*
1 tbsp *honey*
½ cup *orange juice*
1 tbsp *orange zest*
3 tbsp *sesame oil*
¼ cup *vegetable oil*
2 cloves *garlic, minced*
1 tbsp *ginger, minced*
1 tsp *toasted sesame seeds*

Yields: 1½ cups

Place soy sauce, vinegar, honey, orange juice and zest in a medium bowl. Whisk in sesame oil and then vegetable oil. Stir in the garlic, ginger and sesame seeds.

SUGGESTED USE

Shrimp (3 to 4 hours)
Chicken breasts (2 to 3 hours)

SOUTHERN VINEGAR MARINADE

½ cup *cider vinegar*
2 tbsp *Dijon mustard*
1 tbsp *sugar*
1 tbsp *Worcestershire sauce*
1 tsp *hot pepper sauce*
⅓ cup *vegetable oil*
1 tbsp *thyme, chopped*
1 tbsp *parsley, chopped*
1 tbsp *shallots, minced*

Yields: 1½ cups

Mix the vinegar, mustard, sugar, Worcestershire and hot pepper sauce in a medium bowl. Slowly whisk in the oil. Stir in the thyme, parsley and shallots.

SUGGESTED USE

Chicken breasts (2 to 3 hours)
Chicken wings (6 to 8 hours)

SOUTHWESTERN LIME MARINADE

½ cup *lime juice*
6 tbsp *soy sauce*
¼ cup *vegetable oil*
2 tbsp *sugar*
2 tbsp *oregano, chopped*
1 tbsp *garlic, chopped*
1½ tsp *chili powder*
½ tsp *cayenne pepper*
¼ cup *cilantro, chopped*

Yields: 2½ cups

Place lime juice, soy sauce, vegetable oil, and sugar in a medium bowl. Whisk to combine and dissolve sugar. Stir in oregano, garlic, chili powder, cilantro, and cayenne.

SUGGESTED USE

Whole chicken or pieces (8 to 24 hours)
Boneless chicken (6 to 12)
Pork tenderloin (8 to 24 hours)

SPICY APRICOT MARINADE

1 *jalapeño, finely chopped*
1 cup *dried apricots, chopped*
¼ cup *sugar*
2 tbsp *cider vinegar*
2 tbsp *vegetable oil*
½ cup *water*

Yields: ¾ cup

Place apricots, jalapeño, sugar, and water in a small saucepan. Bring to a boil. Simmer until apricots are very soft and mixture is thick. Add more water necessary. Remove from heat and add vegetable oil and vinegar.

SUGGESTED USE

Chicken pieces (3 to 4 hours)
Pork tenderloin (3 to 4 hours)
Pork loin (6 hours)
Turkey breast (4 hours)
Chicken, turkey or pork kabobs (3 to 4 hours)

SPICY BBQ SAUCE

¾ cup *tomato sauce*
⅓ cup *molasses*
3 tbsp *fresh lemon juice*
1 tbsp *soy sauce*
1 tbsp *dark brown sugar*
2 *jalapeños, finely chopped*
2 tsp *Worcestershire sauce*
1 tsp *Dijon mustard*
¼ tsp *red pepper flakes*
½ *Anaheim chili, cut in 1-inch pieces*
¼ *green bell pepper, cut in 1-inch pieces*
1 clove *garlic, minced*
½ tsp *salt*

Yields: 2 cups

Place all the ingredients in a medium saucepan and bring to a boil over medium high heat. Reduce heat to low and simmer, uncovered, stirring occasionally, for 15 minutes. Thoroughly strain the sauce, and discard the solids. Let cool completely and store in the refrigerator for up to 1 week.

SUGGESTED USE

Marinate steak (2 hours)
Chicken pieces (2 to 3 hours)
Boneless chicken breasts (1 hour)

SPICY CARNE ASADA MARINADE

1 cup *vegetable oil*
2 cups *orange juice*
½ cup *lime juice*
4 tsp *red wine vinegar*
2 *serrano or jalapeño chilies, minced*
4 cloves *garlic, minced*
2 tsp *chili powder*
1½ tsp *dried oregano*
1 tsp *salt*
½ tsp *freshly ground pepper*

Yields: 3½ cups

Place oil, orange juice, lime juice and wine vinegar in a medium bowl. Whisk o combine. Stir in chilies, chili powder, garlic, oregano, salt and pepper.

SUGGESTED USE

Traditionally beef is marinated and then cooked until medium rare, cut into strips and served with tortillas, pico de gallo, and guacamole.

Skirt steak or flank steak (4 to 8 hours)

SPICY GARLIC MARINADE

½ cup *rice wine vinegar*
½ cup *soy sauce*
¼ cup *vegetable oil*
6 cloves *garlic, minced*
3 tsp *cayenne pepper*
2 tbsp *dark brown sugar*

Yields: 1½ cups

Place rice vinegar and soy sauce in a medium bowl. Whisk in the oil slowly. Add the garlic, cayenne and brown sugar.

SUGGESTED USE

Chicken wings (6 to 8 hours)
Boneless chicken breasts (2 hours)

Pork tenderloin (4 to 6 hours)

SPICY LIME MARINADE

½ cup *lime juice*
2 tbsp *vegetable oil*
1 *jalapeño, finely chopped*
½ tsp *ground cumin*
2 tbsp *white onion, minced*
1 tbsp *cilantro, minced*

Yields: 1 cup

Place lime juice, vegetable oil, chilies and cumin in the blender or food processor and puree until fairly smooth. Stir in the onion and cilantro.

SUGGESTED USE

Whole chicken (4 hours)
Boneless chicken breasts (1 to 2 hours)
Fish fillet (30 minutes)
Shrimp (1 hour)

SPICY SALTY ORANGE MARINADE

2 tbsp *orange zest*
1 cup *orange juice*
⅓ cup *vegetable oil*
2 cloves *garlic, minced*
1 tbsp *soy sauce*
1 tsp *dried red pepper flakes*
1 tbsp *cider vinegar*
½ tsp *salt*

Yields: 1½ cups

Place the orange zest, orange juice, vegetable oil, garlic, soy sauce, red pepper flakes, vinegar and salt in a blender. Blend until marinade is smooth.

SUGGESTED USE

Skirt steak (3 to 4 hours)
Top sirloin (3 to 4 hours)
Chicken (2 to 3 hours)
Sliced vegetables (1 hour)

SPICY ORANGE MARINADE

½ cup *fresh orange juice*
2 tbsp *orange zest*
¼ cup *lime juice*
⅓ cup *honey*
1 *jalapeño, finely chopped*
¼ cup *vegetable oil*
¼ cup *onion, diced*
3 cloves *garlic, minced*
⅓ cup *cilantro, chopped*

Yields: 1½ cups

Place the orange juice, zest, lime juice, honey and jalapeño in a medium bowl. Slowly whisk in the oil. Stir in the onion, garlic, and cilantro.

SUGGESTED USE

Boneless chicken breasts (2 hours)
Chicken wings (6 to 8 hours)
Pork tenderloin (3 to 4 hours)

SPICY THAI MARINADE

5 tbsp *fish sauce*
½ cup *water*
3 tbsp *ketchup (page 100)*
1 to 2 tbsp *Thai red curry paste*
½ cup *sugar*
½ cup *lime juice*
2 tbsp *vegetable oil*

Yields: 2 cups

Place the fish sauce, water, ketchup, and curry paste in a small bowl. Whisk to combine. Whisk in the sugar, lime juice and oil.

SUGGESTED USE

Shrimp or fish fillets (1 to 2 hours)
Boneless chicken breasts (1 to 2 hours)
Whole chicken (rub under the skin) (1 to 2 hours)

STEAK MARINADE

½ cup *ketchup (page 100)*
2 tbsp *soy sauce*
1 tbsp *Worcestershire sauce*
2 tbsp *brown sugar*
1 clove *garlic, minced*
½ tsp *chili powder*
¼ tsp *salt*
2 tsp *freshly ground pepper*

Yields: ¾ cup

Place ketchup, soy sauce, Worcestershire sauce and brown sugar in a medium bowl. Whisk to combine ingredients until sugar is dissolved. Whisk in garlic, chili powder, salt and pepper.

SUGGESTED USE

Top sirloin (2 to 8 hours)
London broil (4 to 8 hours)

SUMMER TOMATO MARINADE

2 tbsp *lemon juice*
½ cup *olive oil*
4 *tomatoes, peeled, seeded*
4 cloves *garlic, minced*
1 tbsp *sugar*
½ tsp *salt*
¼ tsp *freshly ground pepper*
½ cup *basil, chopped*

Yields: 2 cups

Place lemon juice, olive oil, tomatoes, garlic, sugar, salt and pepper in food processor. Pulse to chop to a coarse texture. Do not puree. Remove from food processor and stir in basil.

SUGGESTED USE

Boneless chicken breasts (2 hours)
Fish steaks or fillets (1 to 2 hours)

SUPER ORANGE MARINADE

½ cup *orange juice*
1 tbsp *orange zest*
½ cup *Grand Marnier*
2 tbsp *Dijon mustard*
¼ cup *vegetable oil*
2 cloves *garlic, minced*
1 tbsp *fresh rosemary, minced*
½ tsp *salt*
¼ tsp *freshly ground pepper*

Yields: 1½ cups

Place the orange juice and zest, Grand Marnier, and mustard in a medium bowl. Slowly whisk in the oil. Stir in the remaining ingredients.

SUGGESTED USE

Whole chicken or duck (8 to 10 hours)
Turkey breast (8 hours)
Boneless chicken breasts (2 hours)

SWEET & SOUR CITRUS MARINADE

½ cup *lemon juice*
¼ cup *orange juice*
½ cup *soy sauce*
6 tbsp *shallots, minced*
1 tsp *dry mustard*
½ tsp *ground ginger*
1 tsp *salt*
½ tsp *freshly ground pepper*
2 bay *leaves*

Yields: 1½ cups

Place all ingredients but the bay leaves into a blender or food processor and puree. Add bay leaves.

SUGGESTED USE

Pork tenderloin or loin (12 hours)
Boneless chicken breasts (2 to 3 hours)
Chicken pieces (3 to 4 hours)

SWEET BOURBON MARINADE

½ cup *Bourbon whiskey*
2 tsp *vegetable oil*
¼ cup *brown sugar*
½ tsp *salt*

Yields: 1 cup

Place Bourbon, salt, vegetable oil and sugar in a medium bowl. Whisk until sugar is dissolved.

SUGGESTED USE

Pork loin (4 to 6 hours)
Pork chops (3 to 4 hours)
Chicken breast (3 to 4 hours)

SWEET JALAPENO MARINADE

2 *jalapeños, finely chopped*
1 tbsp *lime zest*
½ cup *lime juice*
¼ cup *vegetable oil*
2 cloves *garlic, minced*
¼ cup *onion, minced*
½ tsp *ground cumin*
¼ cup *sugar*
½ tsp *salt*
¼ tsp *freshly ground pepper*

Yields: 1½ cups

Place the jalapeños in a blender or food processor. Add the lime zest and juice and with the motor running, drizzle in the oil. Stir in the garlic, onion, cumin, sugar, salt and pepper. Stir until sugar is dissolved, a couple of minutes.

SUGGESTED USE

Chicken wings (6 to 8 hours)
Whole chicken (6 to 8 hours)
Pork spareribs (6 to 8 hours)

SWEET PAPRIKA & RED WINE MARINADE

1½ cups *dry red wine*
3 tbsp *sherry or cider vinegar*
2 tbsp *vegetable oil*
2 tbsp *sweet Hungarian paprika*
1½ tbsp *brown sugar*
1 tsp *salt*

Yields: 2 cups

Place the wine, vinegar and oil in a medium bowl. Whisk to combine. Whisk in the paprika, brown sugar and salt.

SUGGESTED USE

Pork loin (12 hours)
Pork spareribs (24 hours)

TAMARIND GINGER MARINADE

1½ cups *water*
3 tbsp *tamarind concentrate*
1 cup *mirin*
⅔ cup *soy sauce*
¼ cup *golden brown sugar*
2 tbsp *ginger, minced*
4 cloves *garlic, minced*
1 tsp *crushed red pepper flakes*

Yields: 1½ cups

Place water and tamarind in a medium saucepan. Cook over medium high, stirring constantly, until concentrate dissolves. Add mirin, soy sauce, sugar, ginger, garlic and red pepper flakes. Boil until mixture is reduced to 1 ½ cups, about 15 minutes.

SUGGESTED USE

Shrimp or scallops (1 hour)
Salmon (1 hour)

TANDOORI CHICKEN MARINADE

½ cup *plain yogurt*
2 tbsp *olive oil*
1 tbsp *ginger, minced*
¼ cup *lime juice*
1½ tbsp *ground cumin*
1 tsp *paprika*
½ tsp *cayenne pepper*
½ tsp *turmeric*
½ tsp *salt*
¼ tsp *freshly ground pepper*

Yields: 1 cups

Place yogurt, olive oil, ginger, and lime juice in a medium bowl. Whisk to combine well. Whisk in the cumin, paprika, cayenne, turmeric, salt and pepper. Use immediately or refrigerate for 24 hours.

SUGGESTED USE

Whole chicken (24 hours)
Chicken pieces on the bone (12 to 24 hours)
Chicken kabobs (4 to 8 hours)
Shrimp (4 to 6 hours)

TARRAGON KABOB MARINADE

½ cup *olive oil*
¼ cup *champagne vinegar*
2 tbsp *tarragon, minced*
1 clove *garlic, minced*
¼ tsp *freshly ground pepper*
½ tsp *salt*

Yields: ¾ cup

Place all ingredients in a small bowl and whisk together.

SUGGESTED USE

Chicken kabobs (2 hours)

TEX-MEX MARINADE

1 cup *lime juice*
1 cup *orange juice*
¾ cup *cilantro, chopped*
6 cloves *garlic, minced*
¾ cup *vegetable oil*
2 tsp *hot pepper sauce*
¼ cup *chili powder*
1 tbsp *ground cumin*
2 tsp *salt*

Yields: 3½ cups

Place all ingredients in a medium bowl. Whisk to combine well.

SUGGESTED USE

Chicken pieces (4 hours)
Whole chicken (4 to 6 hours)

THAI CHILI HERB MARINADE

2 tbsp *soy sauce*
2 tbsp *fish sauce*
2 tbsp *vegetable oil*
2 tbsp *dark brown sugar*
1 or 2 serrano *chilies, minced*
4 cloves *garlic, minced*
3 tbsp *ginger, minced*
⅓ cup *basil, finely chopped*
⅓ cup *mint, finely chopped*
⅓ cup *cilantro, finely chopped*

Yields: 1½ cups

Place all ingredients in a food processor and process until it forms a thick puree.

SUGGESTED USE

Firm fish fillets (1 hour)
Boneless chicken breasts (1 hour)
Shrimp (1 hour)

THAI CILANTRO CHILI MARINADE

1 bunch *cilantro*
6 cloves *garlic, peeled*
3 tbsp *fish sauce*
2 serrano *chilies*
2 tbsp *sugar*
2 tbsp *vegetable oil*
½ tsp *freshly ground white pepper*

Yields: ½ cup

Cut the top off the bunch of cilantro, which will include all the leaves and some stems, and place in a food processor. Add the garlic cloves and chilies and pulse to finely mince. Add the remaining ingredients and puree.

SUGGESTED USE

Bone-in chicken pieces (4 to 6 hours)
Boneless chicken breasts (1 hour)

THAI CURRY MARINADE

4 stalks *lemongrass (outer leaves removed & root ends trimmed)*
⅔ cup *cilantro, chopped*
½ cup *shallots, chopped*
8 large *cloves garlic, peeled*
¼ cup *ginger, chopped*
¼ cup *brown sugar*
2 tbsp *curry powder*
2 tsp *freshly ground black pepper*
¼ tsp *salt*
¼ cup *fish sauce*
1 cup *canned coconut milk*

Yields: 1½ cups

Thinly slice the lower 2 or 3 inches of the lemongrass stalks and place in the food processor along with the cilantro, shallots, garlic, and ginger. Pulse to finely chop, and continue until as fine as possible. Add sugar, curry powder, pepper, salt, fish sauce, and coconut milk and puree.

SUGGESTED USE

Whole chicken (24 hours)
Chicken pieces (24 hours)
Chicken drumsticks (12 to 24 hours)

97

THAI LEMONGRASS MARINADE

2 tbsp *fish sauce*
¼ cup *lime juice*
1 tbsp *brown sugar*
1 tbsp *sesame oil*
3 tbsp *vegetable oil*
1 large *stalk lemongrass, chopped*
½ tsp *red pepper flakes, crushed*
3 cloves *garlic, minced*
¼ cup *cilantro, chopped*

Yields: 1 cup

Place fish sauce, lime juice, brown sugar and sesame oil in a medium bowl. Slowly whisk in the oil. Stir in the lemongrass, red pepper flakes, garlic and cilantro. Let marinade stand 20 minutes before using.

SUGGESTED USE

Shrimp (2 to 3 hours)
Boneless chicken breasts (3 to 4 hours)
Beef steaks (6 to 8 hours)
Pork tenderloin (6 to 8 hours)
Beef or chicken kabobs (6 to 8 hours)

TOMATO BBQ SAUCE

2 tbsp *vegetable oil*
1 medium *onion, chopped*
3 8-ounce *cans tomato sauce*
½ cup *red wine vinegar*
½ cup *brown sugar*
2 tbsp *Worcestershire sauce*
½ tsp *freshly ground pepper*

Yields: 3 cups

Heat oil in a medium saucepan and sauté the onion until softened, about 4 minutes. Stir in the tomato sauce, red wine vinegar, brown sugar, Worcestershire sauce and pepper. Bring to a simmer and cook, uncovered, until thickened, about 30 minutes, stirring occasionally. Let cool, then cover and refrigerate for up to 2 weeks.

SUGGESTED USE

Use part of the BBQ sauce as a marinade and some as a basting sauce. It can also be used as a glaze or dipping sauce after the meat is cooked.
Chicken pieces (4 to 6 hours)
Boneless chicken breasts (2 to 3)

TOMATO KETCHUP

10 lbs *tomatoes, very ripe*
1 *red bell pepper, seeded & chopped*
4 large *onions, chopped*
1½ cups *cider vinegar*
2 cloves garlic, crushed
1 tsp *peppercorns*
1 tsp *whole allspice*
1 tsp *whole cloves*
5 *cinnamon sticks*
1 tsp *celery seed*
½ tsp *dry mustard*
¼ tsp *cayenne*
4 tbsp *brown sugar, packed firmly*
3 tbsp *granulated sugar*
1 tsp *salt*

Yields: 10 cups

Cut tomatoes into large chunks and puree in a food processor. Run through a coarse sieve to remove seeds and skins. Puree onions and bell pepper and add to strained tomato mixture. Cook this mixture over low heat until reduced by 1/3 to 1/2 and is much thicker.

Simmer all spices over low heat in the vinegar for 1/2 hour, remove from heat and allow to steep. Strain half of this mixture into thickened tomato mixture and stir. Stir. Add sugar, mustard, cayenne, and salt.

Taste the mixture and add more of the spicy vinegar if it seems to be needed. More sugar, mustard, salt, and cayenne can also be added to taste. The mixture can also be cooked longer to thicken to the desired consistency.

TROPICAL FRUIT MARINADE

1 *mango, peeled & cubed*
½ cup *orange juice*
2 tbsp *lemon juice*
2 tbsp *olive oil*
¼ tsp *dried thyme*

Yields: 1½ cups

Place mango cubes, orange juice and lemon juice in the blender or food processor and puree. Transfer to a bowl and whisk in the olive oil and thyme.

SUGGESTED USE

Chicken breasts (2 to 3 hours)
Fish Fillets (30 to 60 minutes)
Shrimp (1 to 3 hours)
Pork tenderloin (3 to 4 hours)

TURKISH YOGURT MARINADE

1 cup *plain yogurt*
2 tbsp *lemon juice*
1 tsp *lemon zest*
1 cup *mint, chopped*
2 large *cloves garlic, minced*
½ tsp *salt*
½ tsp *ground cinnamon*
½ tsp *cayenne pepper*

Yields: 2 cups

Place yogurt, lemon juice and zest in a small bowl. Whisk until smooth. Add the mint, garlic, salt, cinnamon, and cayenne. Let rest in the refrigerator for 24 hours.

SUGGESTED USE

Boneless chicken breasts (1 to 3 hours)
Leg of lamb (4 to 8 hours)

Lamb kabobs (2 to 4 hours)

WHITE WINE DILL MARINADE

1 cup *dry white wine*
3 tbsp *lemon juice*
2 tbsp *Dijon mustard*
3 tbsp *vegetable oil*
¼ cup *dill, chopped*
½ tsp *salt*
¼ tsp *freshly ground pepper*

Yields: 1½ cups

Place the wine, lemon juice, and mustard in a medium bowl. Whisk in the oil and then stir in the dill, salt and pepper.

SUGGESTED USE

Salmon, tuna or swordfish (2 hours)

WHITE WINE SALMON MARINADE

⅓ cup *white wine*
⅓ cup *vegetable oil*
2 tbsp *lemon juice*
1 small *bay leaf*
1 tbsp *juniper berries, crushed*

Yields: ¾ cups

Combine ingredients in a jar. Cover well and shake vigorously. Store in refrigerator until ready to use. Marinate salmon for a couple of hours before cooking. Baste fish with any extra marinade while cooking.

SUGGESTED USE

Salmon (2 to 3 hours)

WINE & HONEY MARINADE

½ cup *dry red wine*
¼ cup *honey*
½ cup *red wine vinegar*
½ cup *onion, minced*
2 cloves *garlic, minced*
⅛ tsp *ground cloves*
½ tsp *salt*
¼ tsp *freshly ground pepper*

Yields: 2 cups

Place the red wine, honey, vinegar, onion, garlic, cloves, salt and pepper in a large bowl, and stir to combine.

SUGGESTED USE

Beef short ribs (24 hours)
Pork spareribs (24 hours)
London broil (24 hours)

WORCESTERSHIRE MARINADE

¼ cup *Worcestershire sauce*
2 tbsp *lemon juice*
3 tbsp *olive oil*
¼ cup *onion, minced*
2 cloves *garlic, minced*
½ tsp *salt*

Yields: 1 cup

Place all ingredients into a small bowl. Stir together to combine well.

SUGGESTED USE

Beef kabobs (2 to 4 hours)
London broil (8 hours)

YAKITORI MARINADE

½ cup *dark soy sauce*
½ cup *dry sherry*
2 tbsp *sugar*
1 tbsp *ginger, minced*
1 clove *garlic, minced*
¼ tsp *salt*

Yields: 1 cup

Place soy sauce, sherry, sugar, ginger, garlic and salt in a saucepan. Bring to a boil over medium high heat and simmer until sugar is dissolved. Let marinade cool completely.

SUGGESTED USE

Chicken kabobs (2 to 3 hours)

Index